Remember Me
and other
VETERAN'S POEMS

Remember Me
and other
VETERAN'S POEMS

Paula E. Provost

To order additional copies of this book, contact:
Xlibris Corporation
1-888-795-4274
www.Xlibris.com
Orders@Xlibris.com
48064

CONTENTS

This book is dedicated to my father,

Arthur N. Provost, who served in WWII,
my mother Lillian L. Provost who put up
with all my writing,

A.I.C. Professor Dr. Gus Pesce for his encouragement

And all the other brave people who put their lives
on hold to Protect and Defend this Nation.

Town of Agawam

36 Main Street   Agawam, Massachusetts 01001-1837

Tel. 413-786-0400   Fax 413-786-9927

Richard A. Cohen
Mayor

April 6, 2005

Ms. Paula Provost
355 Springfield Street
Feeding Hills, MA 01030

Dear Paula:

I am in receipt of your poems and have thoroughly enjoyed the powerful impact they had on all of my senses! These poems are written with a strong message that would certainly be an asset for all to ponder and learn from. Your words grasp the reader and help to enrich their lives by reaching out to other human beings through services to our country. They instill a sense of sorrow while allowing us to be sensitive to the sufferings of others, and responsive to the needs of all people. This in hopes to insure that everyone throughout the world is well taken care of. Then and only then will we all know peace.

Thank you for sharing your poems with me and I hope that you will be able to have them published for all to enjoy. Your poems would have a tremendous influence and leave a unique and memorable lasting impression, now and well into the future. Good Luck!

Very tuly yours,

Richard A. Cohen

Richard A. Cohen
Mayor

Letter from the Mayor of Agawam,
Mr. Richard Cohen

Department of Veterans' Services
Western Hampden District
Town Hall, Agawam, Massachusetts 01001
Agawam Granville Southwick Tolland

Edward A. Kellogg
Director/Agent

(413) 786-0400 Ext. 236/237
Fax (413) 786-9927

April 14, 2005

Ms. Paula Provost
355 Springfield Street
Feeding Hills, MA 01030

Dear Paula:

For some time now I have been honored to be given the opportunity to read your poems. The depth of feeling you convey with regard to the sacrifices our veterans' have made in the name of freedom brings forth a sense of pride to the reader. It has been my pleasure to share these with others, especially veterans and their families. Your words have made them feel proud, as if they truly did make a difference.

I encourage you to continue writing, and certainly to continue sharing. I hope that you will be able to publish a collection of your poems in the near future. Your poetry is a way of reaching out to the community, locally and nationally, reminding us all to support our veterans in whatever way we can.

Thank you so much for giving me the pleasure of reading your work.

Sincerely,

Edward A. Kellogg, Director
Western Hampden District

Letter from the Veteran's Agent,
Mr. Edward Kellogg

CIVIL WAR

Twenty paces we stood apart.
I was sure that you could
Hear my heart.

I know that once,
We could have been friends,
But now our colors say
Fight to the end!

Since I wore blue
and you wore gray
it's true that neither
had a thing to say.

We were given our orders,
must follow them through.
For our colors gave birth

To the Red White and Blue.

ANDERSONVILLE, OUR HOME

How could we allow
A line to decide our fate?
Me to the north of it,
You to the South.

You were my brother,
My neighbor, my friend.

We both thought our reasons were proper.
We both thought our ways were correct.

When we got to this place
Who thought we could do
What man shouldn't do
To another.

Away from here,
In another time,
I loved you.

You were my brother,
My neighbor,
My friend.

No longer does a line
Separate us,
Just the ground
Where we now

REST IN PEACE

GETTYSBURG

A battlefield massacre
A horrendous waste of lives.
The blood of way to many
Men and boys,
Tears of mothers, lovers and wives.

How could Americans
Do to each other
What a line
Gave them courage
To do?

So sad the legacy
Of our "civil" war.
And Who
IS foolish enough
To believe that

War is civil?

THE INFANTRY MAN

We were shipped off to lands
Where the ways
Were not our ways,

And lived in muddy foxholes
For days upon days.

Survival was our daily routine
For things weren't always
As they seemed.

The child who came up to you
Oh, so sweet
Could lead the enemy
To your feet.

Remember your training,
Be cautious of whom you trust,
For to survive from this place
Is an absolute must!

We move forward
Under cover of the night.
Cautiously, stealthily
Up this hill before daylight.

Continued

THE INFANTRY MAN (cont'd.)

Keep an eye on the trees:
Some branches come to life.
With the flash of rifle fire,
You could lose a limb,
Or perhaps, your life.

GOD FORGIVE ME

God, I ask you to forgive me
If I take a life today.

One of the saddest things
About a war
Is the lives that are
Taken away.

Away from their homes
And their families.
Away from the things
They once loved.

But,

Their memories will forever
Linger on.
In the hearts of their families,
And the minds of the soldiers
Who were ordered

To shoot or be shot.

WAR TO END ALL WARS

Since World War I
Was the "War to end all wars"
No wonder World War II is
Forgotten.

And what of all these other
"Encounters," were they just
Conflicts like Korea and
Viet Nam?

Or are they now called
Operation Freedom,
Like in Iraq?

Thousands of people
Lost their lives in these
Meetings, what ever "they"
Choose to call them.

We'd best not forget
The sacrifices made by
Others, to maintain our
Freedom and secure
The same for others.

HELLO AGAIN

Hello again, I saw your face
somewhere in another place.

Another time, another season,
another place, for another reason.

Was it you who brushed my tears away,
as I sat there on that fateful day?

Your comforting hands holding
holding me close as I cried.
Watching those beyond help
lose their dreams as they died.

Though was is hell,
there is peace in death.
From the hands of an angel,

to the voice of GOD.

Dedicated to field nurses, everywhere.

NO WINNERS

There are no winners
In a war.

Just those
Who walk away.

When bodies are counted,
And there's a list made
Of the maimed,

Than "winners"
Requires

A DIFFERENT name!

NO QUESTIONS

A limb for my country
A life for my country

Who knows when it all will end?

Some fought from the water,
Some fought from the land.
Still others fought from the sky.

Things changed so drastically
For those who came home.

How could a Veteran now live on the streets,
Barefoot, sick and nothing to eat?

What happened to honor and gratitude?

A sacrifice was made with no attitude.
They did what their officers told them.

NO QUESTIONS

They went. They fought. Some didn't return.
Our honor was in their hands, Now theirs is in

OUR RESPECT!

continued

NO QUESTIONS (cont'd.)

War is war, bullets and bombs are always real
Can anyone really know how they feel?

Respect and honor needs to, NO, MUST
       replace
Scorn, spit and turned backs.

A Veteran is a Veteran
no matter where he fought for man's rights.

PROMISES

What happened to all the promises
the government made to the Vets?

We'll pay you to fight in uniform,
we'll care for your families back home.

You needn't worry about anything.
We're here for whatever you need.

Just put your life on the line for us,
and face to face take another life.

The life of someone just like you
Who would rather be back home.

When your work there is finished,
Come back home, we'll be here for you.

We'll care for your "ills,"
and shelter you.

We'll even let you use the street for a bed,
and the sky for a blanket.

But your illnesses,
well, they're all in your head!

555th AIRBORNE
THE TRIPLE NICKELS

We stood beside you, man to man
and fought to keep freedom in this land.
We trained as well, and fought as hard in
     combat,
but promotions for us were not to be.

You thought we couldn't be as good as you,
or as brave and courageous with what we
had to do.
But, we proved you wrong,
when you saw how strong,

The Triple Five could be!

We jumped from the same planes as you
and beside you
fought to keep peace in the land.

When our blood ran together,
no one could tell,
was it black, or was it white??

We didn't hold back,
we were side by side
as we dropped into the fight.

Our contributions were
as great as yours
as the blood of the black Americans
also stained the foreign shores.

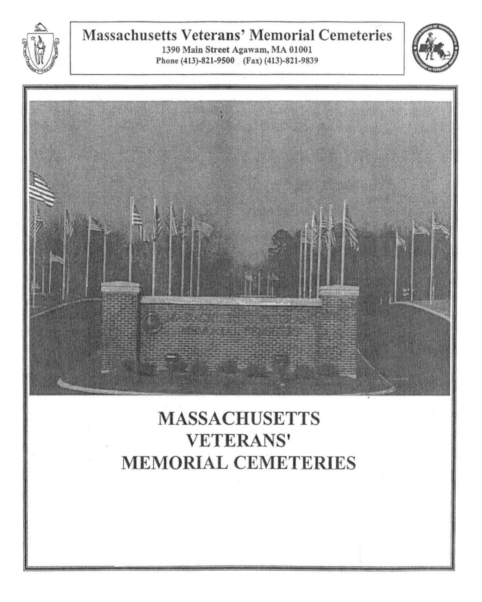

Massachusetts Veterans' Memorial Cemeteries
1390 Main Street Agawam, MA 01001
Phone (413)-821-9500   (Fax) (413)-821-9839

MASSACHUSETTS
VETERANS'
MEMORIAL CEMETERIES

AGAWAM'S ANGEL

Written for Mr. Edward Squazza a farmer
Who donated his land for the new Massachusetts
Veteran's Memorial Cemetery in Agawam.

You gave us a place we can "finally" call home.
A place to "at last" rest our old weary bones.

When medals and ceremony have come to the
        bend,"
they'll parade us with honor, to a great peaceful
        place.
A gift from a man who never went off to war,
who's gardens fed our families while we
        protected
our shores.

His sacrifice, none the less, of our time off this
land.

His loyalty to this country is forever,
No end.

Thank you Mr. Edward Squazza

COLLATERAL DAMAGE

Collateral Damage—
What a horrible category
To be linked in.

Is that all that a human life means?
All that it has been lived for?

When another war breaks out,
And the world is involved,

Will all the elders, women, children
And innocents of the world
Be known as

Collateral damage?

THE KISS AT TIMES SQUARE

The kiss at times square,
Almost everyone was there.
And even those who weren't
Still saw that immortal kiss!

The picture of the sailor,
And the unsuspecting nurse,
Perfect strangers up to that point.

For sixty years and on, the
Symbol, and significance of the kiss
Will always mean relief.

Relief for the families
Whose loved ones had "now" returned.
Returned from a war that once held the world
Captive. An evil war as all of them are.

Maybe someday, with the blessings of God,
Soon, maybe someday,

More families with feel that same relief
As the men and women who are fighting in Iraq
Can return, back to their homeland,

And things will be all right again
With the world.

TRIBUTE TO
POW'S & MIA'S

Please, don't forget us,
we're lost in this land.
In a circumstance
we no longer understand.

We came here together
to give freedom a chance,
but somehow became separated,
were captured or hid.

Lord, help us, we miss you.
We know you miss us too.
But PLEASE, don't forget us,
we're Americans still.

Come find us, we're homesick.
Keep searching and pushing.
We're prisoners, we're bones.

Whatever our conditions,

PLEASE, GET US BACK HOME.

This is written for the MEN and SPIRITS of those who are
still not back in their home land after serving their country.

A VERY "MOVING" WALL

Thousands of names look back at you
back from this lonely wall.
Names with faces known only to those
whose family and loved ones they were.

But can we ever forget their sacrifices?
Sacrifices of youth and life.
Some fought in protest
of a war yet undeclared.

But the bravery they showed
was a Spirit, a Spirit beyond compare.

We'll stand here with tears in our eyes,

Trying to understand how it all came about.
How our young people so unprepared
had to fight for what no-one else dared.

When you come to this wall,
as is hoped you all will,
Remember, Reflect, ask Blessings

For these people, whose lives were cut short.

A PLACE I HAVE KNOWN

I know I've been
To this place before,
But my last time here,
There was a war.

Bodies lying
All over the place,
No age nor religion
No distinction of race.

Just soldiers
Who were hoping
To make it back home,
Lost in this land
Where their Spirits
Now roam.

Remember their sacrifices,
Reflect on their lives.
Take care of the widows,

Whom once they called
Wives.

KOREA

I and II may loom world large,
But Korea DID take place.

If any doubt is still in your mind,
Just look upon the face.

The face of a Veteran who served
In that war.
They're human, and their pain was
Real.
Can you see it there,
How they REALLY feel?

They fought in a war the nation
Seems to have forgotten
With the exception of the 57,000
American families who lost
Loved ones in the war.

Wake up America.
Teach all the wars in school.
A past forgotten,
Is a past destined to repeat itself.

But lessons learned
Have a lasting effect.
Even the one we call RESPECT!

DO NOT DESPAIR

Do not despair, we've not forgotten
for we still bare the scars.

Scars of a war we know took place,
the bombs and guns
were in our face.

We fought for you and for our flag
when we came home,
we did not brag.
The things we saw
will always be there.

We can't forget,
we've lived that life.

The nation seems
to have forgotten all the lives
that have been lost.

But as long as there is one of us
left alive,

WE WILL NOT FORGET THE COST!

THERE ARE NO NONBELIEVERS IN FOXHOLES

When you are forced
To face your mortality
Sitting in foxholes
In Iraq

The mummers calling out
To a higher power
Can be heard
From man to man.

Keep us safe
Make our mission swift
We long for our families
Back home.

I feel sure
That the young men and boys
On both sides
Share this feeling
Of longing for home.

PURPLE HEART

My heart may now be purple,
but my blood's still flowing red.

Some friends of mine
who earned this "prize"

Well, now are lying dead.

We've sacrificed so many things,
Some life, some limb,
Some peace of mind.

But I can tell you this my friend,

World Peace is hard to find.

PURPLE HEART—UNDESERVED

Give it back,
You didn't earn that
Purple Heart.

A traffic accident
Doesn't count.
Only injuries
Sustained in combat.

Oh, since we've already
Given it to you, though,
You can keep it,
But PLEASE, don't wear it.
You've not the right.

And,

We'll expunge it from
Your records.
Keep it and look at it,
And think,
What might have been.

RELUCTANT HERO

Reluctant hero that you are,
Your country has for you,
A star.

Be it silver, bronze,
Or perhaps even gold,
Your gesture of heroism
Did not go untold.

You're duly recognized
For a heroic act
You performed,
Above and beyond
The expected norm.

You showed your country
How brave you are,

So please, From us,

Accept this STAR

REMEMBER ME

We gave up our lives
for yours to be free.
We gave up our lives off in wars,
Why God, ME?

My life had some purpose,
but my country came first.

I had all my dreams,
but to save us the worst,
I went off to a land
where freedom's repressed,
and fought to help others,
'Cause my country's best.

The mud was so cold here,
but the blood ran so warm.

My friends and I died here,
soldiers longing for home.
Hands raised up to Heaven,
God saw us and said,

"Your country will honor you,
the people will cry. When they remember
how many good "men" had to die."

continued

REMEMBER ME (cont'd.)

So love your country, and honor your flag.
Stand up for your freedoms,
to all others brag.
We're free here, we love it
many young people died.
Remember their suffering,

Stand up,

HERE'S THE FLAG!

UNDECLARED

You treat us like we're the enemy,
you laugh at us and pay us no mind.

We sacrificed all of our freedoms,
we gave up all of our dreams.

Our government called us to duty,
and we choose not to run

To protect human rights,
and the freedoms we cherish,
we fought in a war
where many of us perished
and those who came back,
came to a life so precarious.

We no longer had homes,
No place to rest our weary bones,
so the homeless is what
we've become.

No help could we see
was forth coming,
we felt our government
had forsaken us.

(continued)

UNDECLARED (cont'd.)

Our people called us
Baby killers, and spit into our faces,

How friendly is our fellow American

When "you" say it was
"Undeclared"

THE TOWERS FELL DOWN

The towers fell down,
But the Spirit
Went up.

Know this
All you,
Who would try
To destroy
Our nation.

The harder
You try to
Tear down
Our Spirit,

The more you remind us
Of how proud we are
To be called.

AMERICANS

OSAMA BIN LADEN

Osama Bin Laden,
You've joined Saddam Hussein
In becoming a radical terrorist.

Why is it you've become
Such a world hated man,
Did your mother
Not love you enough?

And what of your father,
Did he treat you this way?

It's for certain
Your Allah
Had not a thing to say,
For the Koran teaches peace,
Not destroy fellow man.
Now you've gone and REALLY
Ired a power. A power who will not sit
Idly by and watch you destroy
All that America stands for.
Life, liberty and the pursuit of justice.

Justice for all who do good, or do evil.

With justice, evil WILL fall.

Fall into the depths
From whence you've come.
For we all know for sure,

YOU ARE SATAN'S SONS!

THE KISS

My heart weighs heavy
as your boat
Ships out,

Your kiss
Still on my lips.

I watched until
I could see you
No more,
My tears were falling
On the shore.

I'll pray each day
For your safe return
The love in my heart
Will forever burn.

Dear Lord above,
Protect my love,
Make his mission
Safe and swift.

Please tell him
I'll be waiting here,
With a kiss
Still on
My lips.

Inspired by the deployment of troops to Iraq.

ONE MORE DAY

Another day in the desert sand.
Another hour
with no real stand.

A declaration still not underway
and so we'll sit
for another day.

Practice, Practice.
Keep your senses
alert.

Than sleep again
midst the
desert dirt.

How long must we wait
for some word?
Set to go—

Go home to our families,
or forward
to meet the foe?

STAY TOUGH

Stay tough
Keep on course.

Deal with it
Person by person,
Stay tough.

Your words,
But I notice
You are not there.

Every day, another soldier
Goes down.

How much more
Would you like
American families
To "Suck Up"
For you?

TERROR ALERT HIGH

Terror alert
HIGH

Keep your eyes on
The sky.

But than again
Look to the ground;
Explosives can be
All around.
In vehicles, in people's
Packs,
Some even strap them
On their backs.

If their lives mean
Nothing,
Than ours can mean
No more.
Except for scoring points
As they try to add on more.

Since, (to them),
Life means nothing,

Exactly what is meant by death?

THE SCREAMS

The screams still haunt
When you realize
This is not "practice"
Any more.

The soldier in front of you,
One of your best buddies,
Has just been hit
By an enemy's
REAL bullet.

He's down, he's screaming,
And writhing in pain.
God, what do I do?

"Medic, Medic."
I call for the medic.
But can he get to my friend
Before it's too late?

I've gone over
To help stop the bleeding,
But his needs
Are much more than I can give.

(continued)

THE SCREAMS (cont'd.)

I've moved him, I think
Out of harms way,
But, where is the medic?

I called again,
still no response.
There is one thing left
that I can do for my friend.
I'll ask him to pray with me.

I won't tell him
That his limb is gone.
It's still over there
Where he was hit.
But it's not clean and his life will still work
In spite of it.

After what seemed forever,
The medic is now here.

My friend is going home to his family.

I will stay
To fight
Another day.

BLOOD SOAKED SOIL

The blood soaked soil
Was a constant reminder
Of the conflict
That devastated
The whole land.

The smell of the dynamite,
Mixed with the rotting flesh
Of all who had died
Left such a pungent odor
Hanging in the air,
That our eyes and nostrils
Burned.

How we longed for home
And the sweet smell
Of fresh air,
But, our tour of duty here
Was not yet finished.

Innocent people
Were still being killed
As they trained to hold on to
Their long elusive freedom.

Continued

BLOOD SOAKED SOIL (cont'd.)

How much longer
Must we be here,
To ensure democracy's grasp
In this place?

If ever we craved an answer,
All we need do
Is look upon the face.

The face of the woman
And children
Who were now
Allowed some freedom
Of movement,
Once unavailable
To them.

SORROW'S HANDS

Many of us
Returned from the wars
In bodies
Ravaged by things
We saw and had to do.

When we got back,
Some of us couldn't go home,
for confinement
Only enhanced the pain.

To escape
From these images,
A lot of us turned
To alcohol or drugs.

War really has no heroes,
Only those who survive
And thrive.

Too many people
Pay the price
For decisions
Made by others.

YELLOW RIBBONS

I've seen yellow ribbons
All around
On trees and light posts
In every town.

Yellow ribbons along with a prayer
With wishes of luck
And love to spare.

For safe returns and
And missions won.

Please accept this love
From everyone.

UNCLEAR IMAGE

I wish someone would clear up something
for me.

Just what is torture?
Is it making prisoners undress
And simulate sex acts, or is it
kidnapping an innocent civilian
off the street,
someone who is there to help rebuild
a nation.

Than beheading them
As they beg for their lives
in front of a camera for all the world
to see???

It makes me sad that our soldiers
are court marshaled for humiliating prisoners.
No "real" harm done, except to the psyche.

The insurgent homeland style
Is to behead innocent people
And display the carnage on T.V.

What is TORTURE?
A relative term.

I PRAY THAT I DON'T
LOSE MY LIFE

I pray that I
Don't lose my life
As I go off to take part
In a war.

And, I'd rather not
Take the life
Of someone
I've never met before.

He's done me no harm
Personally,
Nor have I done
Harm to him.

But now a commander say's
It's them or us, and
We must all obey,
Or risk being called

Traitor

**Jeremy Regnier, who lost his life outside,
Baghdad, Iraq October 13, 2004.**

OBEDIENCE

I know I've left a lot behind,
'Cause I wasn't ready to leave.

But the Creator had need of me,
so He called to me by name.

Obedience being part of my trade,

I said "OK Lord, "and whispered a prayer.
For I knew I would not find you there.

I prayed for Him to give you strength
to be able to continue without me.

"Now, not so fast my son", was His answer
to me, "You'll be with them for eternity!
Your Spirit will always be at their side
To give them comfort, peace and guide.

And when their earthly days are through,
I'll bring them home to be with you.

For you are a Regnier, and Regnier's
always come home!"

Dedicated to the memory of Jeremy Regnier

NO CHRISTMAS IN IRAQ

No peace,
No snow,
No gifts in pretty colors wrapped.

Just grenades and mortars
And rifle fire
For the soldiers in Iraq.

No Santa Claus,
No jingle bells,
No wishes well,
They fight in hell!

For families all across this land,
Their lives on hold,
Hearts held in hand.

Christmas time
Will be incomplete.

'Til loved ones return,

From the land of

Tikrit.

The following two "poems"
were written after seeing a news report
on NBC World News Tonight, Christmas Day,
2004.

The reporters were interviewing a
woman and her son. The husband was
deployed to Iraq just after Christmas, 2003,
and killed seven months later.

The reporter asked the child (boy)
"If you could ask your Dad one thing,
what would it be?"

The child thought a while than said
"Daddy, what is it like in Heaven?"
Hence, these "letters,"

DADDY, WHAT IS IT LIKE IN HEAVEN?

December 25, 2004

Dear Daddy,

I'd like to know. What is it like in Heaven?

I know that you went off to war to free some people from Saddam Hussein.

You asked me to be strong and brave til you came back home again. I said that I could do that for you, cause someday soon you'd be coming back home. I kept the other promise I made to you, too. I now have the cleanest room.

I've been real brave, helped Mommy out every day and sometimes even so she wouldn't cry, I took her outside to play.

Today is Christmas, you didn't get to come back home. So maybe I can give you a call and talk to you on the phone. But, when I asked Mommy if we could call you, she began to cry real hard, so I gave her a big hug, she hung on to me tight. So tight I almost couldn't breathe.

She said, Darling, come, we must go sit down
over there and say some prayers with all our might.

We must ask the Dear Lord if He will give your
Dad a message, cause He took him home last
night.

I love you, Daddy. I'll still try to be brave for you.
You know I'll miss you forever, because you're
never coming back to tuck me in at night.

But, one thing I really, REALLY want to know Dad,
What is it like in Heaven?

It would be really nice, and make me and
Mommy feel better, if you could give us a sign,
Or even answer this letter.

I've gotta go now, Dad, Mommy's crying again.
I'll hug her for you, and watch for a sign.
If it would be easier for you, You could send it
on line.

With all my love and kisses forever,

Your child

January 5, 2005

MY DEAREST CHILD

I wanted to answer your letter, but I couldn't do it on line. You see, when God called for me, I left my computer behind. I looked all around, but no one has one up here, there is no need of such material things. After a while, once I am all settled in, the Lord will give me my wings.

But, in the meantime, please know that I am watching over you all. When the good Lord took my Spirit, He left my love for you in your hearts.

Oh, and you know that light a lot of people talk about? It's true!

That is the light that comes from here. My child, the light is so bright and beautiful, you just can't imagine it. And it doesn't hurt your eyes!

As for your signs, whenever you feel the breezes gentle whisper, you'll know that I am there. When you see the lights of the Menorah, or the Christmas tree twinkle, that will be me "winking" at you. Just like I used to do because you brought such joy to your Mom's and my life.

Another thing, I will tuck you in at night, you just won't see me there.

Well, my Darling, I have to go now. But be good, take care of Mom, don't forget your prayers when you go to bed. Remember, I am watching over you and Mom, always.

With all my love, forever,
Your Dad

The local Veteran's council asked me to write a poem for Memorial Day about how you go from a blue star to a gold star. Since we had, just before the asking, lost another local "man" I dedicated this next poem to 1st LT. Travis J. Fuller who was killed in Western Iraq.

1st Lt. Travis J. Fuller killed in Western Iraq
January 26, 2005

A NATIONS SACRIFICE
A FAMILIES PRIDE

I wiped your eyes, and bandaged your bruised knees.
You always tried to hold back the tears.

So brave, I thought, my child is so brave.

As I watched you grow older,
I remembered how brave you were.

The day you came home and said "Mom, I've just enlisted."
I could see the pride on your face.
I thought, I knew you were brave, now the country will know.

The day you left, I couldn't hold back my tears, but I also couldn't hold back my pride. I was so proud of you. You looked proud in the uniform of a nation you chose to protect and defend.

When we went to war, and your company was deployed, we displayed a Blue Star Banner in the window. Everyone knew what that meant. I was even more proud of you now, but also very afraid for you, that is just something families do.

Watching the news became very tense everyday.
Some days I wasn't sure I wanted to keep
watching, but perchance to catch a glimpse of
you I watched.

I worried, please God, don't let my soldier be in
that plane that went down in flames, or on the
ship that was bombed. And still I prayed, don't
let him be in the hummer that ran over the
landmine.

I know that other families were feeling the same
feelings about their children, but I could only
feel for mine, though I prayed for all.

Time is passing, your letters bring us comfort,
but I can sense your growing apprehension in
the way you phrased your words.

I knew you so well when you were young, that
sometimes I could tell these things. No fear,
just apprehension!

You know everyone is praying for you all,
and for your safe return home.

It takes quite a while for your letters to get here
now,
they must be having trouble getting mail planes
out.

'Been some time now, that I've not heard. I
pray you are safe and well.

Dear Lord, I need Your strength, I need You to
hold me up today.
A vehicle is coming down the street, it looks
very official.
In fact military. I'm sure they must be on the
wrong street.
Lord, it's pulled up in front of our house!
The Chaplin is getting out with two other
official looking men.
They're wrong, please go away! Wrong house,
Wrong house I screamed inside my heart don't
come to my door. I won't answer if you do,
Please, don't come here. I know what this
means My Child, My Child, please I would
have felt if something was wrong. Then, I heard
the knock. Oh, Please, Please God, NO!

They've asked me to sit down, and if someone
could come and be with me for a while, and
then they dropped the bomb inside me heart.

It is with great regret that we must inform you.
Your child was killed in a landmine accident
Yesterday.

The rest of their words were a blur. Something about bringing you home, and your belongings too.

But my ears heard none of this. They tell me, "There's a group that meets, they can empathize, because their Blue Star was also changed to Gold.

My loved one is gone, but at least I know this soldier died doing the "right" he chose to do, defending this country.

**Captain John W. Maloney killed in Iraq
June 16, 2005**

KEEP ME IN YOUR HEARTS

Keep me in your hearts,
And I'll do the same for you.

For God has only taken me to my other home,
To the one where I'll wait for you.

My life with you
Has been all I could hope for.
You've nurtured me and given me
A sense of pride,
For family, for home, for country.

It was because of you all
That I became all that I could be.
But my time had come,
Don't be sad for me.

I'm here with my Heavenly "family"

Keep the doors to your hearts open,
And when your time on earth is through,

I'll be waiting here, with love in my heart,
And "open the door for you."

ANOTHER SOLDIER

Another soldier dies in Iraq
As a car bomb explodes
In Baghdad.

Five dead, hundreds injured
When a suicide bomber
Blows himself up in a crowded mall.

A mine explosion kills another
Yet unidentified American Soldier.

How much more of this is the
United States willing to take?
Six more soldiers died this weekend,
Young people whose futures should
Have gone on far ahead.
Every morning when I wake up,
This is the news I hear.

I wait for the day when "the war is over"
Means exactly that, and no one,
Not even an Iraqi dies in this
War again!

WE'RE GONE

We're gone and nothing
can bring us back.

This time we died
In a land called Iraq.

Many more of us died before
in other lands
because of war.

Maybe someday, someone
will get it right,
and stop the insanity
to kill and fight

To bad the world
Has always had this plight,
we want what each other has,
and we want you to do it right.

When everyone is gone,
and there is no-one
Left to fight.

Will we than live in peace,
or end our own lives
'To get it right?'

FOR THE GREATER GOOD

Many innocent will die,
"For the greater good,"
Much more property
Will be destroyed
"For the greater good."

Pardon me,
If I appear
To be ignorant,
For such is not
The case.

But I need to question
The "powers that be,"
For just what is,
The greater good??

I AM A MARINE

I am a Marine, and proud to be,
one of the country's elite.
We're trained and we're tough.
No need to sleep on "fluff"

We're the best that we can be.

Put us out in the front,
we're not afraid to lead the hunt.

You see, we're right
and we're tight.
Always the first to lead the fray.

We're weapons trained so well,

When the enemy realizes we're coming,
they'll wish they were in hell!

I am a Marine, and proud to be
so hear our yell, OO-RAH!

THE SILENT SOUNDS
OF FREEDOM

There is goes again!
Did you hear It?
Are you aware
Of the same sound?

I've been hearing it a lot lately,
Though some days, louder
Than others.

It's taken me a while,
But I've finally figured out
What it is.

It's the sound of hearts breaking
As loved ones die in far off lands,
For the freedom of others.

Not only is the pain felt by the injured,
And those who lie dying
In a land where they would probably
Never, choose to be.

But all their families back home,
Who feel helpless,
When they receive the news.

(continued)

THE SILENT SOUNDS OF FREEDOM (cont'd.)

Fear spreads thru the body
Each time another American Soldier
Is captured, injured, or God forbid,
Killed.

A heart breaks and another silence
Is breached.

I purchased this picture of a soldier at a tag sale in Feeding Hills, MA., in the summer 2005. No one there knew who he was. I have searched, and asked everyone I met both military and civilian. No one knows him. If anyone who reads this book recognizes him I would like you to e-mail me or contact this publisher with the information. My e-mail address is Agawam1@aol.com. I have chosen to use him to represent every soldier, who ever fought in any war. Hence, the title of the poem, **WHAT'S MY NAME?**

WHAT'S MY NAME?

What's my name,
Do you know who I am?
I've fought in every war
Since time began.

I'm every Veteran,
Who ever slung on a weapon
Defending democracy,
And the rights of his
Fellow man.

I'm the soldier who
Never made it back home,
I'm the soldier who's bones
Are in the grave marked
"UNKNOWN"

I've worshiped the Creator
Using every Holy name,
I fought aside many other young men
Who also did the same.

We came from all over
When we were asked to heed the call!
We've been every religion and color,
Some short and some tall.
Some of us were married, and had families

Waiting back home.
Some of us left school to serve.
We proved we "had the nerve."
We had our favorite "motto"
GOD BLESS AMERICA,
LAND OF THE FREE.
Maybe some day, soon, maybe some day
All will be free

This poem was written after a news item stating
that because of an idea of one of the female
Soldiers in Iraq, Favorite bedtime stories were
being video taped as read by the "missing" parent,
and sent to the child at home.
The child could see the parent and hear their
favorite story as well, trying to ease any
abandonment feelings.

BEDTIME STORIES FROM IRAQ

Hello, my darling, I have a surprise for you
tonight.

I know that you can see and hear me, and I can
feel you in my heart.

Are you all ready for bed? Brushed your teeth,
had your water and said your good-night
prayers?

Get all tucked in, and comfy in your bed. Relax
your little head.

Hugs and kisses from me, I love you very much.
Now listen very carefully,

ONCE UPON A TIME—

LaVergne, TN USA
02 July 2010
188127LV00001B/81/P